Musings and A Few Unchallengeable Truths

"When I was your age, I always did it for half an hour a day. Why, sometimes, I've believed as many as six impossible things before breakfast."

Lewis Carroll, Through the Looking Glass and What Alice Found There

To my family and all those who believed in me when I couldn't believe in myself.

www.heatherjanejames.com

ISBN 9781720268437

Preface

The foundation of this book was first published in 2013, off the back of my inspirational facebook page, "Alice in Wonderland's Teatray". Although I very rarely post to the page these days I have never been tempted to close it down for two reasons; firstly that even after I stopped posting I maintained a loyal number of subscribers and I didn't think it very appreciative to vanish it completely; secondly that there are some 3,500 original images and words I produced over a period of 18 months that I think it would be a shame to destroy. Not due to pride I hasten to add, but to the "you never know when it might make a difference" - someone could stumble across something that in that moment is just what they need. The page is still quite frankly of the best things I've ever done. It kept me in a flow of wisdom that certainly wasn't my own, and it was loved.

The Nobel prize winning mystical poet Rabindranath Tagore wrote, "I slept and dreamt that life was joy. I awoke and saw that life was service. I acted and behold, service was joy". I might never have known the wise truth behind those words without my page.

When I first published this book the back cover read;

"I have written from the heart, and everything here is nothing more than my personal expression of what I have experienced and learned. You are free to ponder it or to dismiss it as irrelevant to you. It is very relevant to me. And if one line touches one person in a way that is relevant to them, that brings them a little closer to the light and freedom of life, then this book has served its purpose. I could not wish for more".

The integrity of that holds true today. This is why I write today, why I do anything actually. In the years since I stopped my page I have never stopped working with others to help them achieve a solid spiritual foundation to their lives, I have spent time qualifying in coaching and counselling to support that work, I'm about to start studying for an MA in Philosophy which seemed a natural next step for me and I am close to finishing two books, one on happiness and one on change. Why am I telling you all this? I assure you it's not to gain any false merit in your eyes or mine, but to rather to support with evidence that I'm pursuing what I love, and in doing so I have found it is a love that translates into service.

As I share through writing, images and counselling, the acts I love, I am of true service and rushed with joy. If I had a gift for anyone and everyone it would be the ability to instil that it's ok to do what you love, you love it for a reason, your soul will always be happy following what you love and the whole world will gain. Whether it's building or gardening or studying or being a great parent, a career as a brilliant doctor or skilled painter - it doesn't matter what you love! When we love something we can't wait to do it more, doing what you love becomes, by default, the greatest service to you and all around you. Joyful people create joy around them.

And I love writing. Really love writing. And it's ok to start a sentence with "and". *When you know why the rules are there it's ok to break them* is a frequent saying of one of my favourite mystics of today, the Franciscan priest Father Richard Rohr. I take a great deal of comfort from the words of others - for me all art forms have the capacity to touch the soul. The words you already knew were true without needing any persuasion, the music that dances so familiarly even though you've never heard it before, the picture that you feel as much as see. One soul communicating with another.

Writing was my first love and I expect, outside of my family, it will be my most enduring. I wrote the original version of this book at a time when I had come through an incredibly difficult period in my life, one that taught me the "unchallengeable truths" from which the book is titled. It was written at a time when I was still quite raw from these experiences and as I look back now it's not that I've fundamentally decided what I wrote was wrong - it wasnt, it's called "unchallengeable truths" for a reason! But it was incredibly self revealing in a somewhat naive way that could actually detract from it's topic. So I've edited it, added to it and re-written where necessary and here it is. May it go with you in mind or form and bring a little light to your being!

Contents

Foreward

The original version of this book was constructed using a sequence of ten posters from my page with a short essay behind each. I couldn't even tell you the rationale behind choosing those particular ten, only that it felt right and it seemed to flow together. In this version I have not changed the chapter titles or words from my posters that I selected. You will therefore see each chapter as a title with a subtitle - and in each case these form the basis for the unchallengeable truth to be revealed!

Chapter 1: Happiness

"Happiness doesn't come from having the best of everything - it comes from making the best of everything you have"

If you've got any *ifs* to your requirements for happiness then the sad truth is you may never find it. "I will be happy *if*..." is the most self defeating thing we can say to ourselves, ever! It permanently places us *in waiting,* a state of being at odds with actually being happy.

I pulled an Angel card for one of my best friends recently. I've laughed writing that line, at the outset of my book I've only gone and written a line that could cause trouble! For some reading it won't phase you, for others you could conclude "oh my God, she's some sort of weird hippy chick", take a view about the nature of the book and not read on. Of course I would prefer it that you did read on if you're in the latter camp! Rather than trouble creation however it occurs to me that I have inadvertently highlighted an important idea here for reading this whole book.

The important idea is this: **whatever a sentence suggests to you, suspend judgement**. So much of our spiritual growth and freedom is prevented, thwarted and shut down because we think we know and we judge before we find out. So please, to get the most not only out of this book, but life in general, I urge you: suspend judgement, suspend belief, suspend disbelief! Discover first, decide later. My factual statement that "I pulled a card" isn't designed to convince you of anything, can't harm you and doesn't tell you what I feel about cards, angels or anything else - only that it happened. Anyway, back to the small matter of the card in question. It read,

"Decide to Be Happy Now".

"But I am happy!" declared my friend forcefully. Now I have to say the lady in question happens to be one of the most emotionally sorted people I know, so it took a lot of effort to look her in the eye and say, "I don't think you are. I think you are still waiting". The next day she rang me. "*That card was right, you know. It wasn't that I was unhappy but I was waiting. So today I've been acting. There are loads of things I'd like to come off in the future but you know what, there are loads of things I can do right now and enjoy doing right now too. So I'm doing them. F**k it, I am happy now*". She laughed and put the phone down. So there's the first thing about being happy. It is a now or never scenario.

As I mentioned she's a pretty together (and funny) lady so the step from "not being unhappy" to "happy" is not as far as the one many of us have had, or have still, to make. I've known this woman a long time, and she understands as I do first hand a very different and radical step we must take to happiness. I can still recall what it was like before I knew what that was and how to do it, and it is still with a shudder.

It was a misery I inhabited for many years, living in a state which was not too far off the medical definition of paranoia, the inability to relax properly, an obsession with the thoughts of others, a head that raced permanently. It was constant worry with how I could fit in and get what I "needed"; my job, my family, what I looked like, what I didn't look like, how much money I "ought" to have, didn't have or would require for events way off in the future that may or may not occur, what people thought of me, whether I could or would be accepted. It was accompanied by the dark deep thoughts of damage done to me by others, unjustness and resentments being fed daily by energy from my thinking, whether the original harm was tiny or huge I grew it greater anyway. At the same time I'd be pushing tightly down a huge great lid on my own barrel of mistakes, guilt and shame - lest admitting them even to myself really proved the point I long suspected: that happiness was a sham and even if it wasn't it certainly wasn't something open to me. As those thoughts raced it took yet more energy to keep that lid trapped and tightly shut, excuses, rationalisations, fears, insecurities, race, trap, race, trap, race, trap, racing, trapping... it was exhausting. I'm exhausted writing that. You probably are reading it. But that was my head; every day, day in, day out.

Fleeting relief came only by creating by a false high, a drink, a drug, a love affair, money, a promotion, a change of scene. And then the miserable status quo returned. And it *was* miserable. A short trip down any street in any town shows many people trapped in this misery - many of them trying to do the right thing but still feeling dreadful. I use the word dreadful at its most literal translation: full of dread. Their worries are etched on their unsmiling faces, eyes ranging from shattered acceptance to scurried bewilderment to arrogant antagonism, "what are you looking at?"

Today I have an inward smile outwardly shining. Anyone who looked like that to me when I was miserable I thought of as smug. I didn't know what happiness was so therefore I assumed that anyone who appeared to have it was faking it to prove they were better than anyone else. How sad. How wrong! I experienced no inner joy, inasmuch I believed any who showed up happy was a fake or a liar and certainly arrogant. Or that their happiness was because they had been "successful" where I had failed - a better car, a bigger house, more well-behaved children. "*That must be where their happiness comes from!*" my sickened mind would (convincingly) tell me. I assumed they thought they were superior to me, rather than the truth being that my demented internal condition meant I felt inferior to them.

As my inner life was so bereft I somehow came to the erroneous conclusion that happiness was something I could manufacture if I outwardly got my ducks in a row: career, partner, kids, cash. Amazing what we can come up with with no proof whatsoever isn't it?

The reality is that we can spend a very long time amassing "stuff" and be not very happy at all. The truth is that we can waste our lives living for others - structuring ourselves and our choices not on who we really want to be but on what we think other people think. When I became honest about this I found that others felt the same way. We then wonder why we feel completely empty, our true selves shown no more care than the abandoned on the steps of an orphanage. Anyone else spotted the crazy?

Crazier still is this very western obsession to destroy any happiness whilst it's happening. First we put all our efforts into the manufacture of happiness and then when, in fleeting moments, it drops by, we demean it! Someone asks us if we are happy and we reply "yes, but..." Immediately we qualify the experience; we refer to hardships we have overcome to get here, the fact that we've worked really hard to do it, that it's about time after our loss/trauma/grief.

The subtitle of this chapter reads "*Happiness doesn't come from having the best of everything - it comes from making the best of everything you have*". Most of us don't even realise what we have.

Happiness isn't a thing that needs to be won, it's not something that is deserved and it certainly is not created by external events or conditions. It's internal. It's your right. It exists regardless of what you do. If the Dalai Lama, one of the most spiritual chaps on the planet, can say without irony in exile from his beloved and oppressed nation "the purpose of life is to be happy" - why can't you? I don't know because I've not met him (yet) but I don't think he sits around meditating on the manifestation of a high class item in order to live his happiness. Whenever you see a picture of him he's invariably grinning from ear to ear, so I also don't think he's too concerned with the angle of his chins as the photographer snaps away. I think he does what he loves and loves what he does. In that state we are in a very different level of consciousness, and any of us can be it at any moment.

Happy we are neither self consciousness nor unaware of our selves or where we are. I like to describe it that we are conscious of our surrounding and consciously surrounding. We are aware of what we bring to a situation and we've settled into the space that we have been granted in that moment.

Rumi, the 13th Century Sufi mystic said, "*Your task is not to seek love, but merely to seek and find all the barriers within yourself that you have built against it.*"

We have an odd relationship with the word *love* and use it to cover a multitude of events and experiences - more on that in Chapter 4! For now however I'd ask you to, once you have read the rest of this paragraph, close your eyes for a second and recall being in love, whether that be a moment gazing at a sunset or stars, a child laughing, your lover's voice or touch. It matters not the recollection, only of its tenderness.

For 99% of people the feeling recalled is a warmth that starts in hearts, a warmth that words are inadequate to articulate, a heating, healing peace that is cellular and also all over. In that place you are happy. That's what I am talking about when I talk about happiness. It may or may not involve laughter, it may or may not involve others, but it always starts with love, the universal sort. It's completely within and it's a sensation that is stronger than me of and by myself. That's our right. That's our purpose. To connect with and inhabit that space and take it with us wherever we go - thus usually being happy.

When I was full of fear, dread and worry I didn't know that. I truly did not know that happiness could be mine. Or yours. Just through being alive. Or that both are real.

This does not mean that I now wander around grinning from ear to ear like a delusional lunatic when I am grieving, recovering from shock or trauma or witnessing someone else in pain. It does mean that I stay warm in such situations, and the perpetual inner contentedness is not threatened by outside circumstances. It does mean in the immediate aftermath of such events has passed I am able to be in that space without fear or shame for being it. Remember it's our right, our purpose. The faster I return to it, the faster I can use the events wisely. I am aware that I write in the first person a great deal, and then I interchange it with we or you. It doesn't matter. We are the same, you and I. I'll use "I" to assure you I am not suggesting that you are to do something I haven't myself had to do, "we" to remind you that you are not alone or you to keep reinforcing that we're all equal beings on this planet together.

One of my favourite philosophy questions ever posed is Fromm's "*if I am what I have and I lose what I have, who then am I?*" I'd argue that one of the best kept secrets is that what you truly have is actually something that can never be lost to you.

I've heard many people bang on about gratitude - when you've just lost a loved one, are living in poverty or have serious health problems I'm afraid that's a bit phony, the cart before the horse. Finding something you can appreciate however isn't - and when we appreciate we tap into our soul's desire to connect with our world. We all have the ability to appreciate.

Appreciation is the same energy field as that which creates gratitude so we become connected to it and *then* we are grateful. Gratitude isn't something therefore to be manufactured, any more that we can do so with happiness. Instead we can allow it to roll freely off the back of appreciation. In this manner it is neither forced or false and naturally becomes a practical element of daily contented living, appreciation to gratitude to that warm glow which is happiness.

I mentioned a few situations in which happiness may be more difficult to achieve. Another major psychological block to happiness is that we live in what appears to be a frequently unjust and at other times abhorrently cruel world. *How can I be happy when the world is such a mess?! That can't be right, surely?* I wake up happy and turn on the news to discover that the world has undergone a dramatic shock overnight, a tsunami or earthquake, a war - it matters not whether we consider the event manmade or not. People starving, dying from preventable or treatable disease, poverty, homelessness... are we still supposed to be happy?

Er, yes. Here I urge you to pause. We are all familiar with expressions such as "*you could cut the atmosphere with a knife*" or the or "*you could feel the weight of his confusion*" or "*she lit up the room without saying a word*" Sayings and experiences that are common to us all simply because they are real, regardless of the level of tangibility.

On walking into a room where someone is angry, anxious, distressed, we can feel it. On being close to someone joyful, enthusiastic, passionate, with a light behind their eyes - we too are invigorated. Or alternatively we have visited sites or monuments where an extraordinary amount of human feeling has been expressed; holy sites, memorials, places of miracles and regardless of our beliefs we feel a higher energy, a calling, a peace. It does not take long to imagine our whole planet representing this swirling well of energy, or to conclude that each and every one of the nearly 7.5 billion of us who live here create our own. Which side do you want to be on? Adding to the darkness, the fear or inviting, bringing and sharing the light, the love?

If I accept, at my very core, the unpredictability of life I am then faced with a stark choice. The choice is abject misery at how much does, will and can go "wrong" for ever and ever, or appreciation for the now. There is always something now. Even if you are in the dark days right now you're reading this so you are not in immediate physical danger, that you have this moment in time to spend doing something that is pure and lovely and exactly what you want to be doing without threat. You can appreciate both of those things right now. If you are reading on a bus or a train - look up, you will see someone laughing or a random act of kindness or someone who could benefit from a smile that you can provide - you can appreciate that. If you're outside or near a window look out, there will be a plant or a tree or a bird or a cloud or one of the many droplets of magic nature dangles in front of us daily, or a building that took the hours and attention of many people to create - you can appreciate that. On the good days you'll find yourself naturally appreciative - which is how you were designed to be.

Remember: Appreciation = natural gratitude = happy core.

I have been happy and am happy today because, as I look back on my life, on the lives of others, even my yesterday, or watching the news, I see the first of the unchallengeable truths: **the only change you can predict is that change happens.** The second we attach happiness rather than be happiness, we are liable to lose it. Once the delusion of control or acquisition as a means to happiness is smashed, once you accept that happiness is your right not a reward, once you know that you're doing the planet a favour not a disservice by being on the bright side of life, once you get into the habit of conscious appreciation of your actual reality right now, you can be happy whenever and wherever you like.

Chapter 2: Honesty

"You will never be content living a lie"
"I am a great source of amusement to myself"

Why not tell the truth? It's commonplace not to. We do not tell the truth because we are ashamed of it, we do not tell the truth because we fear judgement of others, we do not tell the truth because it might hurt someone else, we do not tell the truth because then we risk not getting what we want and we do not tell the truth because, like Jack Nicholson ranting in the 1990s classic A Few Good Men, we say to ourselves and others, "You can't handle the truth."

Growing up I was aware that adults lie whilst demanding that children never do. The psychology of lying is a fascinating topic far outside the scope of this short book but in my whole life, I have never understood this phenomena. I've learnt it, I've played it, I've gone along with it. I've used it to my advantage and been disadvantaged by it. But I never *understood* it. Today I do. When we are honest we are powerful. Apropos there's a simply fantastic quote by Marianne Williamson,

"Our deepest fear is not that we are inadequate. Our deepest fear is that we are powerful beyond measure. It is our light not our darkness that most frightens us.".

We lie because it's easier than changing. If you and I are unequivocally honest with each other there is no doubt it would expose some things in us that we wish to change. We lie because without the lie we have no cover and we fear being exposed. We lie to get our own way and yet when others react badly to our lies we stand back and exclaim, look at them, all angry and/or upset - totally ignoring that our lies created the drama. That's the biggest lie of all, that lying helps you or anyone else. In my view it's that *comfortable darkness* that Marianne Williamson so well explains. It does not help anyone however, and I truly know that what is not revealed cannot be healed.

Let's go back to Fromm - "If I am what I have and I lose what I have - who then am I?" In deceit we have no real faith, no love, no courage. The truth is a burning platform for growth and change. The lies are a simmering, smouldering mire, bogging our movements as if in quicksand but never hurting fiercely enough to push us to break out. Our souls however are left aware of the ever present smell. In a lie nothing ever quite *feels right.* We may be outwardly successful, we may have amassed fortunes and families and yet somewhere along the way we lied to get those things. So they never really feel like they are ours, because we do not know if we would be in the same position if we hadn't lied.

Imagine if you never had to lie to be accepted, loved, successful (however it is you define that word). Imagine how much inner confidence you would feel, true security, spectacular peace of mind if you had never lied about anything therefore everything and everyone in your life is there because they chose to be, not because they believed you are something or someone you are not.

And then take a deep breath and know this: you can never be accepted, loved, successful (however you define that word) if you are dishonest. You cannot be truly accepted because you have not truly accepted yourself, you cannot be truly loved because you do not truly love yourself and you cannot be successful (however you define that word) because you do not view yourself as a success.

Many of the world's religions and pop psychologies have gone wrong because they have tried to teach "be this" and then you will be a “good” and “valued” person. They’ve gone wrong because they do not start with what is first.

What if the truth is that you are a manipulator, a people pleaser extraordinaire, a cheat, or a fantasist? What if the truth is you feel so unworthy that each time you gaze at yourself in the mirror you feel little but contempt, pity or desperation? Take that person and give them a set of rules to follow e.g. “thou shalt not kill”, “be kind”, “think of others” and they can do all those things but underneath they still people please, still cheat, still despise their own reflection. Having done all the things they were told would make them a better person deep down they are unaffected. They can pretend to the world to be happy and purposeful but inside they suspect it’s sham - and fear rules. *What if someone found out?*

The pretence takes a lot of effort to keep up, so we are not naturally content or creative because all our energy is taken by maintaining the lie. No matter how good things seem on the outside ***it just feels wrong***. It feels like everything is terribly precarious in a bad way, not at all like my perspective today, the perspective that I hope you have or will come to have too; everything is incredibly precious in a good way.

Why pretend? There can be no movement unless you have a start point, if your start point is make-believe you are never going move into any sort of reality.

Even as a child I knew when things were pretence. In fact I think I became less aware for a while in adulthood, but as a child I used to feel this urge to yell, “stop pretending!” I’ve had this discussion with enough people to know that I am not alone, and that this deep drive for honesty, clarity and truth is within most human beings - no matter how much we have tried to deny it, even to ourselves. I said less aware as an adult, but it came back. It had to. The sham of what I had considered to be life was exposed and ripped apart in all it's glory, except it wasn't a glorious thing. It was gory, unpalatable, painful. Where can you go from that point? Nowhere, or everywhere. I chose the latter and so can you.

Years of guilt and shame do not fall away easily without radical trust that letting go of them will work. There must be a belief that there is good reason to try, that the spiritual power you will receive as a result of the decision to face yourself squarely will happen. The fastest way to feel this power so that you can believe in its reality is to do this, yet perversely you also require some power to do it in the first place! It's a leap of faith. Personally I am a woman of deep faith in God which is very much an experience and does not fall easily into any category; I love Jesus with the same heart that I love the Native American description of the Great Mystery. The Upanishads have guided me as much Carl Jung and Albert Einstein. All of the wisdom I found there lead me, with practice, to my own experience of God. Today that's not a belief, I have no need to believe in something I have experiential evidence of! Neither am I unique in that experience, I have simply followed others and come to know what they knew. It's open to us all.

To have true faith requires a leap into the known unknown: I know there's something but I don't know what it is. On such a path I move freely from *willing to believing to experiencing* but I had to have the faith to start somewhere. So I started with a known unknown: myself. You start with you.

To look at ourselves we must suspend judgement of right and wrong and simply seek what is. And when we look at *what is* we are concerned solely with our responsibility for a chain of events. Responsibility occurs at the moment we decide on a course of action. What about the courses of action we did not decide upon? Those of us who are beaten, abused, victimised, attacked or raped? There is no point asking if you were responsible for an awful thing happening. You were not. The perpetrator was. But there is every point asking at what point you took responsibility for recovering from it. Those who have severe disabilities, illness or debilitating mental or physical health problems? Again working out if things could have been different is a waste of time, but starting from a point of *what is* will establish what responsibility is yours next. What if you are the perpetrator of outrageous harms to others? Then there is every point going back in time - to the point at which you chose to act that way. That's where the truth lies.

It's very difficult to articulate the depth at which we can start to understand our choices from a spiritual perspective - the one I've suggested here is a starting place, to look at responsibility for consciously decided choices. Once this is accepted begins the journey to examine subconscious choices. This deeply spiritual journey may take one to a place where we believe all choices are intended whether you be perpetrator or victim of an act that does not sit rightly within our moral compass, and from there the journey to superconscious or God-conscious selection and manifestation truly reveals itself. I wouldn't suggest to anyone however that they attempt a zero to hero self analysis. Starting the on the path is always enough.

Parts of this chapter are very dark. It is also very real. There is, in my humble opinion, no such thing as fluffy spirituality. An unchallengeable truth: **There is real power for all of us in honesty, and it not is a journey for the faint hearted**.

***

Returning to the start of this chapter, there are two subtitles. I haven't mentioned the second. Why, you may wonder, is "I am a constant source of amusement to myself" up there?

Human beings go to extraordinary lengths to prove their own perfection, instead of accepting another unchallengeable truth is that **none of us are perfect meanwhile on another level we all stand as imperfectly perfect**.

In the original manuscript for this book I included a collection of posters for this chapter - and there was one nestling in the middle about envy - oh, how I loathe it's ugly presence in our lives. There I am, happy enough outside my house when my neighbour rocks up in his spanking new car. Suddenly my vehicle looks cheap, suddenly my house does not look as tidy as his, suddenly I notice how cool and expensive his aviator sunglasses are as he steps out. Whilst I take my own off my head and peer at the unbranded arms, suddenly my chances of getting a new BMW (that's what he's bought), tarting up my house and upgrading my shades are the most important thing on my mind. Ten minutes ago I was happily pulling up daisies and now my energy is of an altogether different variety. I've not moved, but my attachments to what's real have.

We have to learn to laugh at ourselves in this moment to be free! In this moment, I am ridiculous. This moment of despair about owning a car I have no need for, which I had barely considered before, and a pair of sunglasses that wouldn't suit me anyway in comparison to the perfectly functional items I have when some people have nothing it's ridiculous! I am ridiculous! I want it on my gravestone.

The minute I recognise my own ridiculousness and laugh at it, it goes away. Darkness does not like light, and laughter next to love is the best soldier for light there is. After I have finished laughing I may well decide to give my house a fresh paint of coat or consider the car I truly want - all quite healthy. My thoughts can serve me if I use them wisely. They can hinder, not just me but those around too, if I follow them unchecked.

Because, let's take the alternative: what happens if I do not laugh? Well I may start to feel guilty. I ashamedly remind myself how lucky I am, which isn't real gratitude, it's a self induced guilt trip. I may wander over to my neighbour and invent a totally false discussion about how lovely his car is to cover my guilt, a dishonest interchange that leads the neighbour to believe I am his friend when really the sight of his new car (or him) makes me a bit sick. Or I sneer from behind my now unwanted sunglasses, and make some clever put down about his new "drug dealer" wheels... lord, anything! Anything other than just admit, to myself, I'm jealous.

Like all the major emotional states which many consider "bad", there's no such thing, envy is simply a sign post for what we do want out of our lives. Used purposefully it prompts us to follow our dreams, used destructively it destroys the dreams of others and our own piece of mind. In Book 3 of *Conversations with God,* Neale Donald Walsch writes about the 5 natural emotions of envy, anger, grief, fear and love. How many problems are there in ourselves and therefore in our world because we have worked so hard to repress these emotions - rather than experience them and use for their creative purpose?

All well and good but what has this to do with honesty?

In order to be honest with ourselves we have got to lose the idea that there is a right way to be honest. There isn't. Honesty isn't coming up with a clever way to excuse my jealousy in this example, it's simply to admit at least to myself “I am jealous”. It's OK to be comfortable with how pathetic and ridiculous this makes us! It's not a big deal, it's a ‘shruggable’ offence if you like. Such things only become a big deal when we start acting out to cover them up.

If you find the majority of your thoughts in the fearful, resentful, envious, shameful, bitter pile you must acknowledge them. Take them out and have a look, don't pretend they don't exist. Day to day anxieties, well, I bet you could laugh at a lot of them. Once you do, they cannot have a hold over you, you cannot live in fear that you will be exposed as a bitter old being because you'll stop being one. Only if you are honest. You do have these thoughts, accept yourself.

So many of my fears were to do with other people judging me. I wrote them out in a list and I laughed my head off. My fears were: People laughing at me/People thinking I'm ugly/ People thinking I fancy myself/People thinking I'm stupid/People thinking I’m clever/People thinking I’m weak/People not realising I’m vulnerable/People not believing me/People falsely accusing me/Me being overwhelmed by someone dying/Someone dying and me feeling nothing at all... People thinking this, people doing that... the list went on forever! These fears become laughable because am I ever likely to invent a way that enables me to control what others think of me? Ever? Of course not. So these real fears, that genuinely interfered with so much of my life, have the power taken out of them as they are exposed.

If I never admitted I was scared, and what I was scared of, they would have manifested themselves elsewhere; obsessing over where to go, who to see, what to do, which partner to choose... the level of power such fears weald is the real fright. It's like the angry man desperate to control his world for fear of losing it. He beats his wife and children when they stray from how he thinks they should be. Unable to admit he's scared they might leave or not love him he behaves in a way to ensure that them leaving is the most likely outcome, instead of the truth that showing his vulnerability, his humanness might prevent the very thing he fears the most. Every time it gets covered up it, there are occasional murmurings of an anger problem but never about one of fear, so it does not get resolved, and he does it again. The woman so desperate to gain a sense of self worth and escape her guilt that she tries to please everyone in her desire to be loved and respected, or cannot wait to put someone else down to gain false superiority, all because she never let herself feel and grieve the sadness of forced loss of her innocence years before. Bitterness is sometimes mentioned, but never sadness, the real process she needs to allow herself.

Forgive the stereotypes. They're deliberate for ease of identification not because it's only men who are angry or women who are bitter! The man and woman can be swapped in each scenario. It could be anyone, any one of us. It could be me, it could be you.

I am also not suggesting in these last two examples that you laugh at yourself. I said there are two side by side combatants in the force for light: laughter, and the other is love. There are times in all our lives when we must laugh and stop taking ourselves so seriously, and there are others when we need to be kind to ourselves, to know that if we heard our life story from another, we would want to comfort them.

It is the same for all things dark. We refuse to be honest with ourselves because we think, "ooh that's nasty, I can't possibly think like that" - *of course* you can! Human beings have approximately 70,000 thoughts per day. The chances of every single one being a kindly, loving, shame-free, resentment-free thought are non-existent unless you have achieved spiritual mastery. The chances of you having absolutely no happy, loving, creative thoughts are equally slim. Most of us are a mixture, every day, without fail. And it's all part of being human. And it's all OK. The difference between a murderer and someone who has never broken a law in their life may be as fine a line as the latter chose not to act. The murderer fell into a rage and the other laughed at their murderous desires, gave themself a hug and said “it's OK you” to the hurt and angry child inside, “we can do something else today”. Yet both people in this story require healing from their initial thinking, which neither can do if it's not acknowledged. At the moment of honest admittance of where, what and who you are, you become free to move towards your best self.

I know too many people who have created the perfect lie, a nuclear family with social activities on the side. But they don't enjoy this life, they grin and bear it. What they really love to do is read on their own, to swim in the ocean, to go bird watching, stroll naked at sunset. It doesn't matter what it is, but they don't admit to these things because it's not part of the lie. They want a day away every month to themselves because they need space, but the lie didn't create an environment of trust, so they dare not ask. Maybe my neighbour earlier on didn't really want the BMW, he got it because he thought it would help him feel that he fitted in when actually he wanted to take a month off and work on an African mission, but then everyone would think they'd turned into some do-good bible-basher and would laugh at him.

Worse still there are those who are grief stricken by a change in circumstance when they didn't really much care for the situation anyway. It's a double whammy lie! They're living in a false despair over the loss of a life they never loved anyway, a constructed grief over the real death of a false life, a mesh of created realities. There is no freedom to escape it because to do so would mean admitting a lie from the start.

At certain points we will all have what I call a "sliding doors" moment in our relationship with the truth - so named after the film that follows Gwyneth Paltrow in the lead role in two different realities, one having gone through the door and the other not. In such a moment, in all moments, I have come to realise that the universe is hanging on us making the decision, ready to churn it's wheels and cogs once we do. Further I'd add it's always churning, always trying to provide a reality that is better, healthier, more abundant than the one we currently are in. Whichever way we go it churns just the same, but those things take longer to reach us if we've made the task harder through our choices! Nevertheless, wherever possible, make up your heart and mind. In indecision, prolonged waiting, the universe cannot start working on your behalf - spiritually you're holding yourself in limbo and even the "wrong" decision (there's no such thing) is advantageous over no decision at all.

We stay in the dark whilst we are incapable of acknowledging, accepting and seeing the truth. We stay in the dark if we are incapable of be willing to strive for and seek out our highest good, which is always the same course for those around us of their highest good - even if it doesn't make sense to be so.

Yet every day people become capable. They wake up and decide to stop living a lie. Deep breaths required.

It's OK to be who you are. **The truth can never be wrong. It is just what it is**.

This chapter gets many unchallengeable truths! The next is that **being equal in rights and value does not make us equal in experience**. Some people have more trauma than others, some have very little, some are rich, some are poor, some are intelligent, some are dumb, some are funny, some are boring, some are lucky, some lives are scattered with misfortune, some of these are objective comparisons, some are subjective. You could go on forever. The large majority live with experiences at all ends of the scale at some point, yet we judge that some experiences, thoughts and feeling should be lauded and some hidden.

I will not get rid of my anger unless I acknowledge its source; I will not free myself of guilt unless I acknowledge my part in my past, I will not stop judging others until I relinquish judging myself; I will not stop feeling controlled by others until I decide to stop controlling them; I won't know freedom from my thinking until I start concentrating on myself, my thoughts, my actions.

As in the previous chapter, without honesty we also cannot be happy. Honesty requires us to strap the miner's headlamp on and go down into the mental cave, shine light through the darker parts of our being without fear. We must start loving the parts that need love and laughing at the others that need their power taken away.

With self honesty the arrival of humility is spontaneous! I and you are just people "doing their best", and our best varies. It varies of course not just between people but within the individual on different days too. One of my friends sent me a picture message the other day which made me laugh loudly, it said "Some days I amaze myself at my own brilliance, and others I spend hours looking for my phone to discover it's been in my hand all along". Ha!

When we face ourselves we discover an *at oneness* with others we had never imagined possible. Here we all are, human beings, doing our best yet fucking things up and all too afraid to stop and see the truth.

At one time in my life I was hurt very badly by a group of people, a group to whom I had only ever shown kindness and love. I was quite shaken by their attitudes, and an old wise friend of mine said, remember Jesus' last words: "forgive them for they know not what they do". You and I at times in our lives will have genuinely been doing the best we were capable of even though the consequences were terrible. This is the journey through consciousness, forgive us we know not what we do. Once we know that we're ignorant however we then have a responsibility to wake up!

Common misunderstanding of Descartes did us all a disservice by making it widespread to believe that our thoughts are the be all and end all of us. He actually said "I think therefore I am". We do not need to be what we think, in fact thoughts lie! We are what drives our thought, from subconscious to conscious into subconscious again until we smash through to the truth and into superconsciousness - the latter being the beautiful ability to see all those around and yourself with clarity in the big picture.

Today writers such as Walsch, Chopra and Tolle bring a zeitgeist acceptability to Jesus' wisdom of "*forgive them for they know not what they do*" (the Christian church hasn't really done JC that many favours as a spiritual teacher open to all) often remarking that it is vital to remember that each person is doing their best from their current level of consciousness or enlightenment. Allegedly the Buddha was once asked what he had gained from enlightenment. "Nothing", he replied. "But let me tell you what I lost : Anger,

Anxiety, Depression, Insecurity, Fear of Old Age and Death."
That knowing of oneself is worthwhile journey, and it all starts with honesty.

Ah, do you know what. I'm going to add yet another unchallengeable truth, a new one. Just because I can. **It's good to know who you really are, and even better to be it.**

Chapter 3: Kindness

"There are two types of kindness, kindness driven by the ego and kindness driven by the soul. The first one means you will be helpful, considerate, thoughtful and supportive. The second one means you will be helpful considerate, thoughtful and supportive. The first one waits to be loved, recognised, thought of as kind. The second one is an act of service whose rewards lie in inner peace not outward respect. You'll never know which one you're receiving, but you can choose which one to give"

In August 2012 I created a facebook poster that changed my page from a tiny family-and-friends little number to one with a reach of millions and invitations for me to join various inspirational page owner groups. I did not know that would happen and neither was it really on my radar, I was just making pictures and putting words to them as I saw fit in my day. All of a sudden I switched from a total unknown to a page where really big pages were writing and sharing over mine. I was so excited, and also a bit bemused. The poster in question was certainly not the prettiest thing I'd ever made; I think its first version even had a typo! Its words are the subtitle for this chapter.

I understand why it was so popular. There is this view about kindness, that we do it because it's the right thing to do! It is after all, always the right thing to do.

There is a point here where I break with so much that says "just do the right thing". That certainly makes for a nicer planet but it is what I would call "type 3" spirituality, it's a start point.

Yes! if you know what the right thing is, it's a good idea to do it, but the real growth in a person is around their motives for doing the right thing. You could spend a lifetime "doing the right thing" and never be happy, living under the misapprehension that if you do the right thing you'll be treated well by others, that they will give you something back, always waiting for the results of doing the right thing and so common, resenting the people you've done the right thing for.

I have seen too many times the damage caused by apparent kindness that has nothing to do with being kind and has everything to do with the self seeking of the giver. Or the receiver. What? You can receive kindness badly? I'm afraid so. At the outset of this book I spoke of the torture of constantly trying to do the right thing yet always being miserable. If you give only to receive the assumption will be that others do too, and even if they are giving with good motives the receipt is tainted by an either fleeting or more prolonged "well what are they after?"

Kindness given or received in this way leaves both parties resentful in the weight of their unfulfilled expectations. This pure flow that has been given to the energetic field of the world is diminished, instead of its power growing. We forget that to give and receive is an essential part of the beauty of being human, we are individual but not, yet for us to feel connected we are responsible for the flow of energy between us. True kindness has no expectation attached to it, to give and to receive it freely is a skill of equal value. It's rewards are immediate - for both.

True kindness leads to a higher vibration, happier, more loving human being. Kindness charged negatively one way or another can lead to one who is dark and bitter, a lower vibration that not only prevents the individual concerned from experiencing any real joy or peace but tends to drag anyone else around them into the vortex! I call such people "dementors", after the creatures in the Harry Potter movies, the dark entity that sweeps around a room with an open mouth literally sucking the life force out of everything. You might know some! You might unwittingly be one. And that's ok - if you are it's because you've been brainwashed by the "just do the right thing" mentality too; of course you've been left reeling by your lack of inner clarity and peace when you've tried so hard to get it right. You're not alone, but I am going to do my best to help you break out of it, so that you most certainly "do the right thing" but it's not an effort, it's natural expression of an inward soul who deeply knows it's place on the planet.

There was a little mention of "type 3" spirituality a few paragraphs back. As a spiritual coach I deal with "raising consciousness". When I begin working with someone it's very important that I establish where they are and where they wish to go in their spiritual journey before we begin. That's because the real language of type 1, what is more commonly known as Mastery, is so alien to anyone at type 2 or 3 that there is no point using it and hoping some of it rubs off! It won't. The language needs to reflect the common denominators of each level, so that grasping one paves the way to the next. A little like practising finding something to appreciate, and the more you do this the more it leads to natural gratitude instead of writing a forced gratitude list when quite frankly you feel like sh*t!

Case in point is that one of the most prolific level 1 spiritual teachers we have access to in modern history is Jesus Christ, but as such has become arguably the most misunderstood and misinterpreted and misapplied of all messengers. There is no integrity or equilibrium in taking "Love one another" to excuse harm.

I use the words “type” and “level” interchangeably in these next few pages. The types are a way of spiritual teaching, the level is the reflection back of what the person most currently identifies with. I was “given” these descriptions when talking to someone regarding spiritual matters whom it was particularly difficult to deal with. I thought initially it was lack of willingness but it was not, it was pure misunderstanding. As I pondered how to deal with this person who could not accept that the universe did not start and end with his own thoughts yet was also desperately unhappy and wanted to find something more the “types” were presented. I hurriedly wrote them down and, after reflecting on what I had written, have now used them successfully as a way of lifting people through their journey more easily.

As I mentioned, there are three types of spiritual teaching, and thus three levels of spiritual readiness. Who and what sort of teaching you are attracted to initially will be a reflection of where you already are in awareness of your True Self, no level is wrong as ultimately all demonstrate a desire to understand. Some of us have been unconsciously or almost belligerently more forgetful than others.

Fear will define where you are, so with all levels it is fear that we seek to remove. In all the levels there has to be hearing of the truth, and the level you are at is ultimately a measure of your own readiness to accept a truth that is currently not your experience - another was to describe faith. That’s why the most radical and therefore most transformative messages can be so far removed from what we currently know that it all seems a bit bonkers and certainly not something you feel you have the tools to make any use of. Spiritual growth is not so much the addition of new information to create the ultimate spiritual experience, it is removal of our fears, our hang ups, our hurts and our ignorance. Taking these apart reveals the light and guidance of a wisdom we already own. As we progress identification and application becomes easier, the more we know the more we're aware of how little we do!

Starting at Level 3, this is concerned with opening the doors to an experience of higher consciousness but confines that experience to limited parameters of belief, process and knowledge. Level 3 teachings are those commonplace rules of most religions and popular psychology - a framework of ideas or morals that if followed are likely to provide some purpose to life (or at the very least some relief from the suffering or emptiness of it). It is a good starting point, particularly for those with a level of fear which currently prevents a leap of faith. Level 3 is concerned mainly with attitudes, ethics and values. If it is concerned with God at all it is a "hard God" - one that has ideals of right and wrong that a mere mortals such as you and I could never attain but could spend a lifetime trying to. There is nothing inherently wrong with such teachings, and it may well be that aiming at something is better than nothing! Their downside is that following them provides respite rather than permanent solution, and if you don't know that you may well start to feel totally disillusioned and go back instead of move higher!

Level 2 starts to entertain that there is indeed a force within the universe that as a human beings we are party to and can access but shies away from total dependence on that force. It may skirt with experience of a universal peace and power but is still concerned with practices that hone a skill set rather than a total or encompassing experience. It often offers a "soft" God, a God sometimes without the word itself (as if the use of the word may dent its attractiveness). It presents that you can add divine experience into your platter of living with perhaps stretching but swallowable science e.g. the pineal gland in the brain for psychic ability, the genetic presence of the Fibonacci sequence, the link between mindfulness and reduced depression and anxiety. It's a non-threatening approach to spirituality that works well for many, as the rapid growth in yoga, meditation, mindfulness and other tools common to seekers in the 21st Century demonstrates. It accepts that maybe there is another level, a spiritual paradigm which we do not so much see but we can experience. It is not so concerned however with the constant and perpetual experience of it at all times and all moments.

Level 1 seeks to know God, without placing any human conception or religious barriers to the understanding of that word - part of our liberation towards knowing God is to remove the hang-ups and preconceived ideas we have around the word itself. It is the path that requires the leap of faith, a way of living that is as comfortable in not knowing and nothingness - the very thing that at level 3 we are trying to avoid.

Many of us suspect Level 1 is there but do not find the necessary revelation to tap into it with any real or sustained commitment. Don't give up! A glimpse is followed by another and another until one day, whoosh, you're living in the longest deepest safest glimpse you couldn't even imagine. Concern only with your deepest connection to your innermost self and the experience of the divine within you is something as pragmatic as breathing.

When we stumble across something that speaks the truth so clearly that we cannot fail to hear it, we may pause and think, wow. There is a fabulous Hindu word for spiritual wisdom which is "shruti". It does not have a literal translation in English, but it would come close to "heard" or "received" wisdom. Here we have the work of great Prophets and Masters, often we can trace the start of any religious tradition to one of these. It is the language of the mystics, so often condemned or dismissed in their own lifetimes. The musings of Rumi, Hafez, St Teresa of Avila, Julian of Norwich, St John of the Cross, Meister Eckhart, Zohar, Dante, Tagore.... I cannot do a just list here but each spoke of union with the divine that was more akin to the ecstasy of mind blowing sex and drug taking than sitting in a stone building once a week or reading a book.

The most radical and therefore most transformative messages have come from Level 1 teachers. In being so they are therefore the messages that from a judgemental ego state are the easiest to dismiss.

Yes all very interesting but this is a chapter on kindness! And indeed there is, I feel, not the room in this book to further delve into how religious, spiritual and psychological teachings can help or hinder us through the journey described here, so I'll get back to the topic in hand. The purpose was to create the pause that says where am I? So that actually we can then say, like Alice in Wonderland, where do I want to go from here?

Where are we with that? When the current Dalai Lama said "my religion is kindness" I believe he was showing us a way to be that opens the doors for the compassionate flow of love between all humans. It is something naturally felt at level 1, I have no sense of separateness here, I know that harm I cause to myself or to you I cause to all, love I give to myself or to you I give to all, that my tiny little presence as one of seven and a half billion souls walking the earth can and does make a difference.

What does that mean practically? An example might help. I used to make a cake for a weekly meeting I attended. One week someone said to me "you're only doing it for your ego, they won't like you any more or less just because you make a cake". When the people pleasing card was levelled at me I was quite honestly surprised. I had learnt enough of people pleasing to know that that wasn't what I was doing at all. I simply wanted other people to feel a bit of love in that group. I made my cakes with love and purpose. And the person who had nothing better to do than dismiss a nice gesture (exposing far more about themselves than me anyway), was wrong. I wasn't people pleasing, thinking these people will like me if I make them a cake. I thought I was being kind. Yet I did have an expectation.

After my father died, I still went to the meeting. As I walked in, within my ear shot, someone muttered, "we'll see if she's still happy to make cakes and be so nice now won't we?". I felt like I'd been struck. It was 5 days since my father's death, I'd held his body. I couldn't believe this woman was so cruel. There was my error, my kindness was exposed as still having an expectation. I didn't expect people to like me just because I was bumbling around being nice, but I didn't expect them to hate me either.

It's a hard, hard lesson. You can be the most decent person in the world but if doing the right thing doesn't generate worth in yourself, by yourself, for yourself, it will not add value to your life. I am not advocating for a second that we all give up and start being mean! I love to be kind, to help, but I only do it now because I am grateful to be of service. It connects me, awakens me, energises. I have no expectations that it will somehow protect me from the others being cruel. What it does do though is enable me to respect myself, so that cruelty of others hurts less.

Internally we are shielded and supported. The flow in and out of us and through us is stronger because it's not intended to stop.

Respect for our own worth is the greatest protection we have; all by itself. If I value myself by what I can bring, I get to sleep with a clear conscience.

This little story about kindness was nothing compared to trials I later went through. For me my journey has very much been that having been pushed to witness my own darkness it was as if I had an urge to really understand more and then sought it out in others. It would take me a month to go through in words the conclusions one can draw from that! I do not regret the learning the circumstances I have placed myself in to do so enabled - but I wouldn't necessarily recommend it either.

A few years ago my children were traumatised by a series of events that exposed to me just how dangerous one person can be. As a family we reeled and ultimately became stronger but at the time I could barely function, and any doubts I had about the damage mean spiritedness can materialise were wiped.

I describe this period in my life as feeling like a dog that has been run over. I was nearly dead, but not quite, and I would manage to crawl to the curb and whimper at a passer-by, perhaps someone I had always wagged my tail at before. And they would look the other way, unable to see my broken form, and instead of just walking on, would give me a kick, back into the road, where I'd be hit again by an oncoming truck. These were people I had only ever been kind to.

I have no judgement for the people who were unable to help me. It is a spiritual truth that we will seek to deny, rationalise or minimise the pain of someone else if we have yet to deal with our own. I am still kind, I'd gain nothing by belligerent refusal to be so! I try to never, ever expect anything in return, and rarely when it seems that I did indeed have an expectation that I have unwittingly or unwillingly denied or rationalised it is usually exposed and it is me who suffers. Our choice is to give freely or give not at all.

In my experience some of the kindest people in the world are those who have been hurt the most too, and have learnt from it. They are able to understand the impact of even the smallest word or act, whether good or bad.

We can of course ask for kindness too. Sometimes we will get, sometimes we will not. Being kind when we can with no expectation is something we can do for one another for no other reason than we can. To not do it when we can feeds the insecurity that cries we are each worthless, to do it demonstrates that no one ever is. The unchallengeable truth? **Some people will treat you badly whatever you do, so whatever you do, do it for you.**

Chapter 4: Love

"We all have it"

I truly believe that what distinguishes us as human beings is our capacity for love. Love is more than an emotion, more than an attachment, more than a desire to protect, more than a feeling. It is a sense of power and a sense of purpose. It is uncommon wisdom, guiding, safe, warm. When we are loving towards another we are not lost, when I am being loved by another I am found.

This capacity to love exists independently to any physical or emotional attachments, the capacity to love and be loved is always within us, regardless of the relationships we are in. By default, therefore, my capacity to feel love is a part of me and part of you. This capacity is actually is permanently within us. I have it, you have it.

So where is it?

Firstly I'm aware, and not for the first time, that language limits us! As a child I was fascinated by Chinese writing. It's written language is "*logographic*" - which means it has no alphabet and represents a total word without spelling - bang - straight into your brain. I wish we had a symbol for the love that we're talking about here that could do the same! Our social media sites are awash with love-hearts, mine too at times I hasten to add so there's no judgement, but sadly there's no alternative either! For me they always look a little bit silly valentine, slightly immature, somehow inadequate against what we're talking about. Love is the spiritual superpower. Boom. It's not some frilly little pink notion of sentimentality, it's courage, it's conviction, it's comfort, it's expansion, it's secure and it's freeing, it's being held and being empowered to move at the same time, it's simultaneously having solid foundations and wings to fly, it's an experience and a state of being, its always there but it requires choosing, its constant *and* in flux, it's paradoxical, ambiguous yet totally consistent, it's everything that matters and *in* everything that *is* matter... it's... **so much more than a four letter word!**

Open any magazine, novel, newspaper, social media site and the word "love" is all over the place. "I love him more and more each day" proclaims the recently dating actress, "I never thought I could love anyone so much", says the musician of his new son, "I thought our love would last" sobs the newly divorced reality star. Is any of this to do with LOVE? And contrast with the rather brilliant if slightly-disturbing-to-the-British-establishment sermon by the American Preacher Reverend Curry in the wedding earlier this year of the Duke and Duchess of Sussex. I have to confess I remain in the "don't steal the limelight from the bride and groom" camp in terms of the length of time he banged (literally, pulpit thumping and all sorts) on for but the message itself? Reverend Curry's address started as follows:

"*The late Dr Martin Luther King, Jr. once said and I quote::* 'We must discover the power of love, the redemptive power of love. And when we discover that, we will be able to make of this old world a new world, for love is the only way.' *There's power in love. Don't underestimate it. Don't even over-sentimentalize it. There's power – power in love. If you don't believe me, think about a time when you first fell in love. The whole world seemed to center around you and your beloved. Oh there's power – power in love. Not just in its romantic forms, but any form, any shape of love. There's a certain sense in which when you are loved, and you know it, when someone cares for you, and you know it, when you love and you show it – it actually feels right. There's something right about it. There is something right about it. And there's a reason for it. The reason has to do with the source. We were made by a power of love, and our lives were meant – and are meant – to be lived in that love. That's why we are here*".

Wow. Bear with me... *if* God is love, and God being love is within, and God speaks through people - what better platform could that God use than a wedding watched by over 50 million people at the time (according to Forbes). Today I suspect many more, as it left the Rev. Curry an unlikely YouTube superstar!

All communication rests with the ability to transfer an idea from one mind into another and be understood. It's no wonder that we're wondering where it is when our messages on *what* it is are so inadequate and inconsistent. Perhaps that is how it should be, that the mystery must remain alongside the knowing that exists without explanation. Perhaps.

I'm at pains to explore what "love" means. As a word it's slipping into our collective conscious more and more yet simultaneously we're running the risk that the deepest, mythical, powerful and most enlightening messages that use the word love are getting lost in translation.

I was not surprised when coming across Miguel Ruiz's Four Agreements, a beautiful book containing the tenets of Toltec wisdom, that the first agreement is "*Be Impeccable With Your Word.*" So, as with any word when the meaning is open to misinterpretation, I'll hit the dictionary. Oxford English, in order to be precise. Except when I did that with the word *love* I left not being any clearer. To save you the same excursion I'll just say that there are twelve different definitions, it is a noun, a verb, an adjective, an adverb and an attributive or adjunct noun. No, it's not simple. It can be do to with a strong affinity for something, an attachment to it, a responsibility toward welfare and sex. Amongst other things.

The conclusion has to be therefore that love is a word of many meanings! I've used the word a few times in this book already, to describe my feelings for people or activities. I don't wish to change my use of the word nor suddenly decide to not love such things just because I'm pushing here for a metaphysical definition of the word. I just have to understand that love in spiritual terms is not that idea of affection for something.

It is rare that the dictionary fails, but alongside this brilliant tool I'll often look at the etymology of a word as signpost. So that's next! The word love comes from the old English "lufu" in a definition I have to say, I, er, love; "to cherish, to delight". Do you cherish the people, creatures activities or things you say you love? Do you delight in them?

Lufu itself is a Indo-European word, coming from the Germanic *lubo* and Sanskrit *lubhyati*, and Latin *libet*. The Latin and Sanskrit versions share an interesting perspective as their translations are approximate to "desire". There's a word we're probably more in consensus about what it means; "yearning, longing, craving, wishful needing". As background to the word love it sets us upon a course of reflection that perhaps in matters of love we are seeking, searching for, wistfully dreaming of something that will complete us. That completion is love itself.

Love in this sense appears a great deal in all the major religious and spiritual traditions. There is an incredible verse in the Upanishads, the foundations of which are believed to date up to 1000 years BC if you believe widely accepted history and one million BC if you think we've gotten our commonly taught timelines wrong (yes, I said a million. There's a great deal we don't really know for sure).

"As long as we think we are the ego,
We feel attached and fall into sorrow,
But realise that you are the Self, the Lord
Of life, and you will be freed from sorrow.
When you realise that you are the Self,
Supreme source of light, supreme source of love,
You transcend the duality of life
And enter into the unitive state.
The Lord of Love shines in the hearts of all,
Seeing him in all creatures, the wise
Forget themselves in the service of all
The Lord is their joy, the Lord is their rest,
Such as they are the lovers of the Lord.
By truth meditation, and self control
One can enter into this state of joy
And see the Self shining in a pure heart"

I personally do not find any departure from the messages of the New Testament, "God is love" or "the kingdom of God is within" in these words. How very wise the Upanishads appear to be in that further they are suggesting you must be able to isolate and do battle with your ego to feel this love?

Not long ago I met someone who said, "I think that the devil that Jesus faced in the wilderness was his ego." It's not the first time I have heard such an argument, it was the first time I gave it any serious consideration. So back to Jesus briefly - who was clearly an ego free man as self sacrifice is the ultimate lack of ego and I don't think that anyone could argue against the level of sacrifice of a man who preached only peace and love for one another and was crucified for his efforts. What if there are lessons in here that we are missing in the biblical story of the forty days and forty nights? The time Jesus spent in the desert is a story of temptations. Is it not true that each time I am "tempted" to respond to someone based on my own fears or insecurities I am acting in the darker side of human nature as opposed to living in a way of love? Is it not true that I am "tempted" to, I don't know, have a fling with someone who is married, lie about my income for tax purposes, scream like a banshee at my kids, I am being "tempted" into behaviour that my conscience would tell me is wrong? If I then follow what Jesus said when he came out of this battle, that God is love and the kingdom of God is within, was he simply telling us there's a much better way to live, which is beyond judgements and in peace and joy? Perhaps this story of biblical temptation over forty days and forty nights should have a bit of a renaissance, as a metaphor for our own internal egotistical struggles.

I stumbled across the evangelical preacher Joyce Meyer not long ago. I couldn't recommend highly enough her writings on "The Battlefield of the Mind" and hope that doing so also demonstrates to anyone thinking I'm being disrespectful towards a certain religion that I'm not. Yet I am also not afraid to consider what religious messages actually mean to me - I have blind faith in God not religion. So, she and I do not share a religion, and I'm not suggesting she would agree with my musings above, yet her experiential Bible led teachings on mind and ego management are quite frankly brilliant. As I hope I've managed to achieve throughout this book, I am not trying to convince you of anything, it's simply to prompt contemplation!

Whatever, it is, without doubt, my ego that keeps me from love in the power sense. What a sweeping statement that is! Yes, it is, but it's also true, and acceptance of it is also the basis of any humility in my life. My ego judges, compares, analyses but invariably it's drivers are fear and control not love and service.

So what is the ego? A quick flick though any search engines of the word "ego" will give three key aspects to its definition. Ego is the Latin for "I" so we're talking about the you in your body, as distinct from other bodies. In Freudian psychoanalysis terms the ego is the part of our psyches most in touch with the external world, governing our conscious thoughts and behaviours in relation to it; and finally it is about how we view and feel about ourselves; the good view being one of balanced self esteem, the grandiose view being one of our own self importance. The question is never whether egos are relevant or not – they are, it's what weight we give to them that determines our level of suffering. Once you know that jealousy or guilt for example stems purely from ego – it's easier to deal with and you can look fearlessly at it and heal.

As Deepak Chopra states, "If you want to reach a state of bliss, then go beyond your ego and the internal dialogue. Make a decision to relinquish the need to control, the need to be approved, and the need to judge. Those are the three things the ego is doing all the time. It's very important to be aware of them every time they come up."

If I am unaware I cannot move away from my small self, ego self into my true self which already knows love in that powerful creative manner. I find it interesting that the Buddha didn't like the word love very much, highlighting some of the issues discussed here about defining the word in a sentimental or attachment driven way. For instance I cannot love something or someone that I fear to lose or need to control. Buddha sidestepped the rather frustrating "many definitions of the word love" debate entirely and instead he asserted that the force felt through enlightenment was one of a self sacrificing benevolence and purpose, called *metta*. That's the power one.

Without knowing that I have this capacity, life would be a very disheartening deal indeed. One where I am in constant battle to be a *have* over a *have-not*. All those manic thoughts, some good, some bad, some downright ugly and all based around what I can get to make my life worthwhile.

What about what I can give? With no love the world would be full of self centred raving lunatics, maybe in some parts of the world or your life it is but it doesn't have to be. Love is the anchor point. As soon as we get our heads around the fact that love exists, or that our capacity to experience love exists, independently, permanently, we learn and then we know that we can call upon it at any moment. It's not something we have to fight or tread over others to get - it's something we have already received. Maybe that's the purest simplicity of the God is Love messages.

Love exists regardless of my circumstance, simply waiting for my willingness. My willingness comes when I am unafraid. The relationship between love and fear, and their mutual exclusivity is covered masterfully in a Course in Miracles, but if that's too tall an order to study just bear in mind that you cannot love when you are in fear. Worrying about people you care about is destructive and not a sign that you are in love, rather one of fear. I always advise worriers to turn any worries into a prayer - before they've finished forming the concern! "What if someone attacks my...." is turned into "Love, please keep my child safe" before it's complete. "How will I pay for...." becomes "Love please fill me and guide me so that I can provide."

Love is everywhere. And anywhere. Like magic, we can conjure love with a simple flourish of our hearts. That's something available to all human beings, from any religion, from no religion, it's already mine and yours.

Even with the most limited experience of love we all have an idea that love enables us to do miraculous things for one another, courageous things, selfless things. That flicker of love in a new romance or gazing at a beautiful sky... just the beginning! There's no ego present in those moments that's for sure.

When we then acknowledge it's omnipresence in our lives, incredible things happen. It is the permanent difference between me having a reason to live and a reason not to. Indulge yourself, follow your dreams, to stop and stare if you wish, forgive yourself as you would show compassion to someone else, to know you are love, loved and loving. Life is lived in love in yourself and shared with others. That is something worth fighting for, something worthwhile to believe in. So here is the unchallengeable truth: **in the experience of love people can do amazing things.** You know it's true! You can achieve the unimaginable if you feel love. If you really don't feel it, the best place to start is to get that ego in check, have no fear and be of service to another in a truly altruistic sense. That's when your superpower will be revealed.

Chapter 5: Discovery

"This is your life. No-one else should live it on your behalf"

This is the only chapter in this book where I'm undertaking a complete turnaround, a total 180' departure from the original tone. For starters I'm going to begin with the unchallengeable truth. The unchallengeable truth is this: **we shall be constantly learning and changing until the day we die, things that worked for us once will not work for us always, and we can never guarantee an outcome, only what we put into the process.**

That truth has not changed. Which is handy as they're supposed to be unchallengeable so one would hope they'd stand the test of a few years if not lifetimes!

However I know that large parts of this chapter I had written from a perspective which is at odds with so much of what I am trying to address: freedom comes from discovering your innermost, highest self and then being true to it. The first time I wrote this chapter I was not true to myself. Please bear with, and I'll try to explain why!

Originally I used the subtitle: "Anyone I know of with a faith that really works for them did not get it by being told what to do or to think, they got it by being given the freedom to explore their spiritual selves". When I wrote it I didn't *not* mean it, but I didn't mean it in the way it was shared massively by pages I respected who I wanted to respect me. So as the comments and likes and discussions appeared I not only allowed them to continue on a basis of misinterpretation but then I also used the post's popularity in my book. Seriously. And that's just a load of old bollocks.

It was one of the reasons I removed the book. It always stuck out to me as pandering to ego led spiritual sickness, instead of standing up to it and saying actually, do you know what, sometimes we do have to push aside our own prejudices and ideas and be prepared to accept the advice of those that have gone before us.

You can, if you wish, forever say "I'll not have anyone tell me what to do". It's a position that an ego would like to think of as a strong one, powerful even. I'd ask instead why you think stubbornness or closed mindedness is an asset? This is the ego at its best, convincing you that if you open your mind on spiritual issues you are somehow the victim in a conspiracy. Perhaps you will be coerced against your will into a set of beliefs that are not really yours. Well here's the belting blow: it's only your ego that is under threat by exploring ideas.

The more awake your soul the less your ego has control of you, and boy does your ego like control! It wants your soul to stay asleep because then it reigns supreme. Your soul's job is to be of service, to you and everyone around. A soul is never threatened by exploration, how can it be? Simply by picking up this book, any book on spirituality or religion you run the risk of your ego going "uh-oh! I've been rumbled. Quick! Think of something utterly convincing so I don't lose my power". It's the same ego that will never follow up on wondering what Joyce Meyer talks about as I've already said she is an evangelical Christian preacher and your ego (fear, effectively) says, "she might convert me! She hates all gays! Even mentioning her is tantamount to brainwashing". Did your mind have the same reaction when I mentioned Buddha? Probably not, he's got a better rep than most Christians. Although if you're a Jehovah's Witness you'd be as horrified by my mention of Buddha and ideas of Jesus battling his own ego as the average reader may be about me extolling the virtues of an evangelical preacher.

I am thankful for every religious and spiritual writer who has put pen to paper. I pick things up to read, pretty much the way you are reading here I suspect, and I might not value very much at all except for one sentence. That one sentence is all I need to give me a different perspective.

There is something I am party to, have experienced and therefore know to be true. It is the ageless wisdom, that invites all and excludes none, principles, ideas and understanding that I know now to be in the perennial tradition. I don't have access to it because I'm different to you, I am the same. It is simply that my life and circumstances lead me to a point where I had to clear out, remove or retire large portions of the small me, my false egoic self that thought I needed a particular home, car or school for my children, a certain amount of money, a particular group of friends, to be accepted in a specific class. In order to be held and exist in a higher level of consciousness, attachments to them had to go. Not everyone reaches the point, and certainly not many reach the point willingly, I know I didn't! All I know is that once that point is passed there seemed little option but to accept there might be something more than the box I had created for myself.

Quite simply the pain of ignorance became greater than the pain of holding onto what I knew was shallow and untrue, and I became willing to hold onto absolutely nothing.

I actually drew a deep breath upon writing that, and felt the goose bumps ripple across me from the inside out. I became willing to hold onto nothing.

In return I received an unshakeable foundation that no man, beast or circumstance could remove. Pretty cool and it's yours too. There's always more being revealed, and it's rather exciting. But do you know what else? I absolutely got it by being told what to do by those who had done it before me.

I would not have learnt anything if I had not been willing at certain points to do what I was told, and I would not have learnt anything at all with a closed mind. This is your journey, your voyage of discovery and you must own it but without the ability to not believe everything you think you'll never broaden your experience. I will never tell anyone what to believe, but I will say that experience does not come to us by sticking with what we believe we already know. We must be open to discover that which we do not.

Years ago I read Alain de Botton's *Religion for Atheists*. Despite it not really being what it says on the tin - it's more a platform for de Botton's ideas on how we might ignite greater moral passions in our secular world - it's a great read, and I'd recommend it to anyone; atheist and believer alike. However, having finished the book what struck me most was that in all the arguments that de Botton, a self-confessed atheist, so eloquently made for the adoption of decent spiritual principles into the lives of non-believers, what he actually gave me was a description of the God which he so vehemently denies. Why? Why can this obviously bright, spiritually aware man of rather decent literary standing not bring himself to use the word "God" as a point of reference? He's not alone, nor I hasten to add am I arguing that he is wrong. Each of us has a right to believe as we see fit, but this animosity to the word God is commonplace, does not a derisory approach to a small, three letter word make proper investigation of what the ancient traditions offer more difficult than it needs to be?

De Botton argues that the secular society has a great deal to learn from the faiths, all faiths, and that just because we can't accept the God as described by any particular religion doesn't mean that we should avoid the tenets which are most fruitful to a happy human existence. "Spot on Alain!" you could almost hear me cry as I read. As he rightly observes most religions aren't too keen on their followers treating it as if it's "a buffet", from which one can select the bits one fancies! He says, "but why not?" So do I! If Buddhist or Hindu meditation practices work for you – why not learn from them? If belief in the healing power of Christ works for you, why not pray to it? If letting go of resentments and making amends is a practice you believe believe you would benefit from why not use the principles set out as part of Yom Kippur? Our atheist de Botton then goes onto describe how we might benefit from engendering deeper spiritual principles of love, kindness, art appreciation, meditation, looking at the darker side of life... Everything he describes is what God is to me, so I finish the book thinking "how strange, Alain and I believe in exactly the same things, we believe they are essential for happy living, yet he is adamant there is no God and I am adamant that he's just described mine..."

So, what's in a name? That's all we're left with. I talk to a lot of people about God. An obsessive prejudice against the very word itself is frequently the biggest stumbling block in launching into a new spiritual experience. I'll be damn certain that no human being is capable of defining God, which is why we have so many different variations on what he/she/it might be. Underlying each attempt to bring us closer to the source is a rake of societal, cultural norms of the moment which add the human factor, the ego factor, and then we've got something to argue with. We end up discounting a whole religion for one sentence, rather than developing an understanding of our truest and deepest natures for ourselves by learning from the experience of our ancestors. How exhausting that humankind is unable to bring into its evolution with any real conviction the messages of wisdom that have revealed themselves to so many through the ages! Don't let the ignorance of others, myself included, on their somewhat blurry or ineffectual descriptions of their own experience of connection with God put you off seeking your own. Anything that makes you a happy more purposeful human being has got to be worth it! Even ardent atheists do not discount that people have a spiritual aspect to their beings, so don't let someone else's description of what God is prevent you from exploring that side of you!

I have needed to discover. To discover I needed to let go of the ego driven fear that someone was trying to tell what to do and allow myself to be helped, led, healed. I can't do that if I judge the information as unnecessary to me before I even look at it! I've needed to roll things around and contemplate, to try it out and see if it works! I won't do that if I'm convinced that I can't learn anything more. If you're reading something like this you're already wondering if there's something more or you wouldn't have picked it up! So don't lie to yourself. You cannot on the one hand say you have a desire to learn and on the other stand back like a three year old with folded arms saying "don't tell me what to do". No-one is. There's an extraordinary amount of spiritual guidance out there, and within us, if we're willing to try.

I'm always discovering. In fact this book is representative of how that little voyage of discovery happens - I started from a position that I was miserable and didn't know what happiness was and somehow I've ended up experiencing a very real God or source of love and light power in my life, stumbled across wisdom that I just know is true from across the ages (when previously I would have dismissed it as nonsense so something is at work in me), learnt that I'm not alone in this process and discovered a real joy in helping others on their voyage. Just today, someone started a conversation about Stoicism, and I learnt new things to mull over which may or may not add value to the way I operate in the future. We certainly cannot regret learning more whatever happens, and at no point can we afford to be threatened by simply exploring something that is new to us.

Discovery never stops. I believe that quest for knowledge, by default, has to be never-ending. There may well only be one truth, but how you get there could not possibly be the same for all. I don't claim to know it all, I am not writing here as in this is the way to do it! I am writing here to share things that I have learnt which may help you or someone else. That's all. You're in the driving seat.

And in the driving seat you must remain. A journey of spirituality is the greatest gift of our lives. On face value our lives are nonsense, we are born, we do stuff, things happen to us, we die. That may be enough for some, for me and many others it's not. I don't doubt of the existence of spirit, for why would I question whether there is anything more if there wasn't a part of me that believed there was? I wouldn't have any call to.

One thing I would add is that I try to steer clear of debates as to whether man created God or God created man, as they're fairly irrelevant to the purpose of starting the journey. Today I have to admit to fairly strong views on the subject but I also have to admit I might change them! Never let pride standing in the way of growth. The whole point of this spiritual exploration, for me, is to live in a way I enjoy, where I feel I have purpose and value.

I am a parent. If nothing else my purpose is to parent my children. What's theirs? Who knows. Did Alberta King know who her son would be? No. So this comes first. And secondary to that I just do. I take decisions to house, clothe and feed my children first. If I fulfil no other role this is enough.

I have found that marvellous things happen in my life when I keep an open mind and do the best I can with what's in front of me. That is the journey for me. My religious and spiritual views have changed and strengthened and developed as I move through life. Those I know who are content and I have this in common: that through accident, trial, error, taking advice, going off on a jolly of our own; through discovery we have found something that works for us, that we love, and that we do not take for granted.

Chapter 6: Intuition

"Listen to your inner voice"

I have made many posters about intuition. I have called it "nature's warning signal", anything I wrote such as "my soul and yours are very old friends" or "some people we meet we already know" were always quickly popular on my page. These experiences we share as human beings, are, for me, simply further proof of my existence on a spiritual level. They do not have to be for you! Yet the resonance these posts create and the volume of their sharing suggested that intuition is a very real experience for a great many of us.

In the absorbing "*Blink: The Power of Thinking without Thinking*", Malcolm Gladwell writes; "Our world requires that decisions be sourced and footnoted, and if we say how we feel, we must also be prepared to elaborate on why we feel that way. We need to respect the fact that it is possible to know without knowing why we know and accept that - sometimes - we're better off that way."

Yet how, and why? In the science of my personal experience the best outcomes in my life have happened when I trust my gut feeling. The place where I live I knew nothing about when I moved here, yet I felt absolutely convinced and compelled to move my family to it. I was easily able to justify the reasons to anyone who asked but ultimately it was because it felt like the right thing to do. Everything fell into place to enable us to move and as a result of that decision my children experienced schooling I could only have dreamed of, in fact if I did dream of it it is what they have received, we have all made the best of friends, the balance of life has always been good here, it is *home*. We truly did not put much effort into it being so, it is like it already was.

On my last trip to hell I ignored my intuition. No one made me do it. Of course the devastating consequences I could not have foreseen, I had no frame of reference for the horror I was about to witness, but there is a point, a turning point in my existence where I felt I should do one thing and I did another. I paid a dear price for that, and for a long time wallowed in a loss of sense of self. There is therefore a moment where I accept my responsibility for what was about to unfold.

Rather bizarrely I ended up in a position with what appeared on the surface to be very similar circumstances some years later, and despite my fear and everyone around me reminding me of the previous situation, this time my intuition told me to see it through. It was not easy but my peace of mind was protected and I learnt an aspect of myself I might otherwise have missed. We do repeat until all the rot is uncovered and removed! Our role is to trust that intuitive guide from a higher source and act upon it.

The greatest threat to intuition is rationalisation. Whether you believe intuition comes direct from God or is simply a by-product of human sensory overload isn't my business.

The oddest thing about intuition is we always know when we have had it. I'm sure I'm not alone in saying that for large portions of my life it might have well sat in the box marked, "hindsight".

After an event we proclaim, "*I had a feeling this would happen*" or "*I knew it would turn out like this if we carried on*". The last time I lost my temper with someone things had been popping up, niggling and nagging me for weeks. Now I didn't know that I'd not have my finest hour in that situation but I did know something was amiss - and that knowledge was correct, the facts exposed afterward revealed things were actually worse than I felt!

If, as a human being, one of our gifts is an in built prophecy function, why would we not choose to use it more wisely?

For me the intuition question is wrapped up in the relationship between the mind and the soul, the conscious and the subconscious, another one that harps back to the ego and the being. The majority of my conscious thinking, until I become more enlightened, is primarily that of my ego - what it wants, what it thinks it deserves, how it thinks things should occur.

It can't be said enough, although I've certainly tried in this book: egos want control. The lack of listening to intuition, the much more deeply felt "I must be wary of that" or "I need to focus on this" is easy when it fits in with what our ego tells us we already want. It's also easy to follow if it seems rational.

Our problems arise when our intuition and our egos are giving us conflicting messages. Our intuition whispers or even screams, "It's no good for you here! Get out! Now!" and our ego says, "but this is everything you've ever wanted so you can't leave!" And then, years of rationalising our fears kick in, and the internal dialogues take over. We hear only the training and orientations we've inherited and developed since childhood "oh you never know what you're doing/you've been wrong before/don't be too hasty".

No wonder intuition is so frequently ignored when it is competing with so much noise. For me the trick of utilising intuition for it's best purpose is to practise listening to it, to tune in to it, to give it freedom to be heard and opportunity to be considered. It takes time to learn to trust your inner voice; time and commitment.

We can all benefit from getting to know ourselves better.

The first thing to examine is our major orientation(s). These are the personal truths we hold to be self evident, worldviews which we start framing in childhood. Fear of abandonment for example is a very specific orientation dealt with at length by psychologists and pastors alike. A view of a whole gender or race based on the action of one and cemented by the action of a few others create commonly occuring orientations of racism, ageism, classism, sexism. A boy growing up with a belief that "all women cheat" is an orientation that will leave every female companion in adulthood tearing their hair out to prove it's not them, or indeed he will subconsciously seek those who cheat to bring into his life thus proving his world view correct. *Men always put their work first, I am unworthy/stupid/destined to fail, fat people are kinder than thin ones* - it could be anything! You'll know it's an orientation because it's a deeply held belief on the way your world works that is based upon a flimsy and sometime logic defying rule - yet we frame major decisions based upon it. Hence all women cheat is simply untrue, some women cheat is accurate. But try telling that to the man who believes it is true and has devoted his life to proving himself right. Your orientations will shape your internal dialogues which in turn will shape your ability to listen to your inner voice. Once you know what it is, you must also know that that is *not* your intuition.

What else can we consider *not* intuition? Well it will not magically tell us what others are thinking, it may pick on what others are feeling depending on our empathy tuning, but those are grey areas. That's not intuition's purpose and not necessarily to be trusted without proof.

It will however definitely and truthfully be telling us what we are thinking, feeling and experiencing at our deepest level. Even if our minds are covering that up with a million and one convincing lies. Intuition is deeply personal to each of us. Egos will try and rationalise, justify and tell us that we know what others are thinking so that it, in turn, can rationalise and justify its own motives and actions. Intuition is always trying to protect, help and guide us to the best choices and decisions for our highest good, therefore the good of all.

In *Blink* Gladwell demonstrates the accuracy of this sixth sense through a series of examples and stories, and science. This sixth sense is arguably more accurate than the more familiar five of sight, sound, touch, smell and taste which we do not take as they are either by the way! The very simple foundations of the communication psychology NLP offer great evidence here in the dangers of this battle of discernment and a sound argument for trusting your gut. NLP states that from our initial start point of sensory experience our minds will then deny, distort or generalise the information we are receiving in order to determine an appropriate response. We have denied, distorted or generalised a sensory experience from our five human perceptors anyway based on, you guessed it, our egos and orientations. Why not trust the sense that is potentially less biased than the rest?

Intuition is that voice that says "do it"/"don't do it". It's that simple. It's your conscience, your moral compass, your inner you. You are still free to ignore it when you like. I still do, foolishly, although much much less frequently than I've ever done before. I am learning, slowly. There are some areas of my life where I have become exceptionally adept at listening, and somewhere I haven't. I know which ones are working out best!

One more thing. Mainly because it's super interesting! Well, I thought so anyway. On my flyers for my coaching business I use a quote from renowned American astrophysicist Neil De Grasse Tyson, "Everyone should have their mind blown at least once a day!" Well this is the stuff that can blow your mind, as one of the questions it may lead you to asking is if you truly understand where your mind is!

For some reading this book the words *chakra, manipura* or *kundalini*, will be familiar, and having got thus far in the book with only references to more traditional spiritual gurus you may well be delighted that they're about to make an appearance. For others they will be words with a new age connotation, for others still having only just gotten used to me chucking around the word God as if there's no tomorrow and asking you to trust that believing Jesus knew what he was talking about does not mean you've converted to Christianity well then, this might require a wet flannel and some smelling salts. But hey, ho, nothing ventured, nothing gained. So just like before, I'd ask you to suspend whatever you think you already know which may leave you open to discover something new!

The discovery of DMT, a chemical compound identified in 1931 and labelled "the spirit molecule" by Dr Rick Strassman's book on the topic in 1996 exists in trace elements in humans, animals, birds and plants and its bodily production has been linked, but not yet proven, to the pineal gland, also known as the "third eye". This pine-cone shaped gland found in the brain is oddly depicted in ancient Egyptian hieroglyphs as the doorway to enlightenment. DMT is believed to be responsible for collective consciousness inter species, explaining why birds fly in formation or human beings have access to shared wisdom.

Chakras appear in depictions of human spirituality throughout the ages. Starting at the base of the pelvis and moving up to the top of the head they have different colours, vibrations and meanings. There are seven bodily chakras (let's save out of body chakras for another time) or energy circles, said to exist through the core of the human body, and the energy required to activate and balance them is called Kundalini. The Ajna chakra is often referred to as the gateway to God or the third eye. They appear everywhere from ancient civilisations and hinduism and even modern day medicine; the use of the Caduceus, showing two entwined snakes around a staff with wings is said to be an original depiction of Kundalini energy as it begins at the base or root chakra and works its way up the spine. Certain forms of yoga are the practice of releasing this spiritual energy through the body. (Interestingly the Caduceus is not permitted in India for use as a medical symbol because of its identification as representing Kundalini, instead the sign is supposed to be one snake around a rod, imagery from the Ancient Greek myth of the rod of Asclepius. The're a lot to suggest the world's a smaller place with a more deeply entwined history than we realise!)

Another of the energy centres is the Manipura, the one located at centrally just behind the navel and allegedly responsible for emotions, wisdom, state of being and feelings attached to what the third chakra picks up. Consider it in the context of "trusting your gut" or "gut feelings" and that for me is when lots of things start to go boom in my brain. More fascinating still is the increasing scientific evidence suggesting that we do indeed have a "second brain" in this area of of our bodies. As yet we seem unable to identify exactly how the relationship between this gut sensory message system and the brain we all know is in our heads actually work together, but the second brain is believed to be responsible for a large number of preceptory and reactive functions.

There is a lot of information in those paragraphs. It's not supposed to be a scientific argument for or against anything one way or another. It's just a small snippet of the curious synchronicities of wisdom old and new that's out there. Along with the other areas looked at with regards to understanding what is intuition and what is fantasy however it has a good use - the simple exercise to start observing ***where*** feelings, thoughts and ideas arise from within you.

The more time you spend in quiet, it does not have to be full blown meditation (although I am a big fan), the closer you will get to understanding what all the different levels of noise are. Just giving yourself five minutes peace each day of still contemplation, to discern what is what - this is a practice which brings you closer to following your deepest and highest guidance.

It seems that intuition, its nature and presentation has absorbed the best thinkers, scientists and, dare I say, magicians for as many years as man has existed. The unchallengeable truth in all this? **Intuition is a very real experience for a great many of us, and it never tries to harm us.**

Chapter 7: Awe

"Somehow the recognition of how small I am, can make me feel really big"

This is my shortest chapter. A decent view has always had the power to take my breath away. Whether of hills or beaches, mountains or lakes, a road that seems to run forever, a building that reaches the clouds, a flower that springs in a concrete jungle - It matters not. These things have always affected me. I once made a poster of my dog lost in thought, with a magnificent vista as the backdrop. The slogan read, "on the hills I contemplate Pantheism" - the school of thought that says the divine source is present in everything especially nature (of which Einstein was a great proponent).

I lost my awe for a while. We can lose it. Have you got yours? It's as essential as breathing.

The best thing about awe however is, that like appreciation leading to natural unforced gratitude, it is something you can practise. It is something you get better at the more you do of it! It is something that you don't just wait to have flood you (although if it does, enjoy... throw your arms in the air and inhale), it's something you can go out and get.

I have never been anywhere in the world that there wasn't something to wonder at. Ever. We get so busy, walking to work, running our homes and households, rushing in to do something here, do something there, yet one of the greatest parts of life for me is how amazing it all is. To stop and stare. What a luxury! How fortunate I am that my senses can experience this.

I am not going to say much more. Get out. Start looking. Every day for a month make a conscious decision to stop and stare at something small like a flower, change your planned journeys to include a scenic route and stop and get out, take pictures. So many of us have decent cameras on our permanently carried mobile phones these days! What a great way to start being interested in and engaged with the everyday surroundings! I feel like a permanent tourist some days... there's just so much to see. Celebrate the planet. Consider with incredulity both feats of nature and triumphs of man. Anais Nin said “we don’t see things as they are we see things as we are”. True, but perhaps truer still is that we can turn that around and benefit. Decide, yes decide, to see things as they are. They’re amazing. With this practice starts to enable the flow into you that says you are amazing too.

An unchallengeable truth? **There is beauty everywhere**.

Chapter 8: Courage

"Grant me the serenity to accept the things I cannot change, courage to change the things I can and wisdom to know the difference"

That's a commonplace version of the first few lines of The Serenity Prayer. Today it is frequently attributed to US author and theologian and Reinhold Niebuhr. It's a prayer that has used, changed and popularised over the years, most notably as the closing prayer for 12 Step fellowships the world over thanks to its adoption by Alcoholics Anonymous in 1941 as its founder Bill W observed "never had he seen the spiritual programme of AA summed up in so few lines". Niebuhr's full version is:

God, give me grace to accept with serenity
the things that cannot be changed,
Courage to change the things
which should be changed,
and the Wisdom to distinguish
the one from the other.
Living one day at a time,
Enjoying one moment at a time,
Accepting hardship as a pathway to peace,
Taking, as Jesus did,
This sinful world as it is,
Not as I would have it,
Trusting that You will make all things right,
If I surrender to Your will,
So that I may be reasonably happy in this life,
And supremely happy with You forever in the next.

It's adoption by such organisations as AA stems ultimately from a principle of spiritual growth found in doctrines the world over, which is one of personal responsibility. That's my sweeping statement but here goes with the mind blowing stuff again: It's been found on walls dated back to the 15th and 16th Centuries in as far flung places as California and Russia, and on a Egyptian obelisk dated 2000 yrs BC. Reinhard himself said of such discoveries,"'of course, it may have been spooking around for years, even centuries, but I don't think so. I honestly do believe that I wrote it myself." I honestly believe he believes he wrote himself too, and I honestly believe that he wrote it tapped into this source of wisdom and power that this whole book has been hoping to express is available to all.

Commonly in such groups it is used to remind people that the only thing they can truly change is themselves - for those hoping to recover from mental illness and addictive conditions this is of course essential - if I am an addict, alcoholic or anorexic on suffer with one of the many mental and spiritual conditions these fellowships offer reprieve from, the temptation to concern myself with the affairs of others or indeed things that are outright not my business may kill me. At that point I am of no use to anyone. As such it's a simple and brilliant reminder to focus recovery on the internal state of individual, not the individuals external circumstances - wise advice for us all.

Having included Reinhard's full version however I think there we can see a small, yet very relevant, anomaly between it and the abridged version. The difference is in the insertion of the word, "*should* be changed". Well, I think it's clear immediately why the word is frequently omitted! My version of what "should" be changed may be very very different to yours. A brief shoot back through the history books shows time and again of mass atrocities committed and led by a few individuals who thought they knew what "should" be changed. A world in which everyone is running around thinking they have the right to change anything for personal gain whilst others suffer is a dangerous place.

That same history however is also littered with great leaders of change that positively affected thousands, millions and left the human race better for it. If Mother Teresa or Nelson Mandela had not decided to change the things they thought should be changed where would we be?

I think Gandhi got it right when he said, "*be the change you wish to see in the world*". Here we have a leader who, like the earlier mentioned Martin Luther King Jr, sees change not as a violent struggle where one has to lose in order for another to gain. It's a peaceful path of demonstration and love that excludes none but does not stray from the greater good. The hindu word that sums up this approach is Ahimsa, which translates as nonviolence and compassion. It's founded in the karmic ideal that as a human being, each one of us being a representation of the greater source, harm to one is harm to all.

If we blur the lines about what we can change, we look at the part that says wisdom and consider if we are wise. I'm afraid I have to admit to getting the giggles at this point of rather serious writing. What I share here I'm still practising myself and on this particular subject in some aspects of my life I am brought right back with a bump to "I am ridiculous". It's been my experience that I sometimes don't know how wise (or not) I am being until after the event. That's my wisdom: I don't know that much at all! Ha.

I digress. Courage for me, is another of those elements of being human that exists, independently of us as a resource, like love and awe. I watched Hacksaw Ridge not long ago, the film of the saving of 75 soldiers by pacifist Desmond Doss in the Second World War. I sat in utter admiration of the fact that in faith that there *is* more, more comes. Who can forget the unarmed and unknown rebel at Tiananmen Square in 1989, the emergency services in New York on 11th September 2001, Martin Luther King Jr "having a dream", Malala Yousafzai escaping the Taliban to campaign for the rights of schoolgirls' education not just in her native Pakistan but the world over?

These are extraordinary events. What about those whose normal circumstances are so difficult that each day requires an act of courage? Carers, parents of those with disabilities, the homeless? Acts of courage required just to keep going in each day. My experience is that when I have relaxed into it, which is a really odd turn of phrase, it comes. Not forced, allowed.

We forget it's there, we forget how to draw upon it until pushed into a set of life circumstances where we have no choice. Surely there is an option for us to draw upon it each and every day?

In that five minutes space I take each day to listen to my intuition, to discern what is really going on for me, I often ask for courage. I did this morning. Courage to finish and publish this book, courage to take a decision I've been putting off. You can ask too. You do not have to have a labelled source, you are simply asking.

Daily we see extraordinary acts of courage by ordinary beings. They come from the young and the old, the rich and the poor, the healthy and the sick. Courage is not a club with rules of entry. Like all spiritual gifts courage is another that makes no judgement on whether we are worthy enough to be endowed with it, our circumstances, ambitions, past or abilities must not fit a specific set of criteria in order to activate it. Activation comes at the point of recognising we need it, ask for it and using it.

I receive daily contemplations from the Centre of Action and Contemplation in New Mexico run by Richard Rohr, just a brilliant contributor in my humble opinion to world spiritual health. Rohr often talks of accepting that we do not receive the benefits of spirit because we are worthy, he is fond of saying, "God does not love us if we change, He loves us so we can". Rohr's starting point that we are all equally unworthy is a difficult pill for many to swallow, but I get it. Humility has real power. Whenever I have humbly asked for extra power to do something, that it is a wise thing to do, and doing it will not cause harm to myself or others whoosh, it is there.

In one of those oxymoronic ways that something makes sense but shouldn't - a paradox that defies logic there is a massive correlation between levels of humility and levels of courage. Courage can be defined as, "the ability to do something that scares one, bravery", which it helps to contrast with self-confidence "a feeling of trust in one's own qualities, abilities, judgement" (yes, more recourse to the dictionary!) When we are confident we are doing something we already believe we can do, when we are courageous we are involved in the unknown. Thus if humility is a sincere understanding of what and who we truly are, lacking any pride or arrogance, it then follows that to receive the courage we need we must start from an admission that we haven't been able to do or get it yet. Remember turning worry into prayer? *"I am so worried about that..."* becomes *"I ask that I may be given courage to change this..."*

My unchallengeable truth is this; **human beings are capable of extraordinary acts of courage**. Be that the dramatic rescue executed in the face of disaster, or recovery from a sequence of tragic life events, we are capable. If human beings are capable of extraordinary acts of courage and you are a human being, then you qualify as being capable.

This very real relationship between humility and courage means that through accepting that human beings can do incredibly courageous things, where is my humility if I do not believe this can also apply to me? I *can't* we say, *why can't you* says courage? Why are you so different to those who can? You're not. Only your fears or pride and that dratted ego would have you believe otherwise. There's another unchallengeable lurking here: **that any human experience can be experienced by any human being**.

It takes courage to let go, it takes courage to forgive, it takes courage to admit when we have really screwed things up, courage to move on, courage to chase a dream. In living a life where I would like to be happy, and I want to listen to and act upon the guidance from my inner voice, courage ceases to become an option and becomes a necessity.

I have learnt that courage is like a muscle, it responds well to exercise and training. I often think of the analogy of learning to swim. It is not until you push off into the water, until you jump in, that your realise you are not going to drown after all. It is not until you try, that you know. But once you know that you are not going to sink after all, you must then get on with learning how to swim well. You need help, you take lessons, you ask others who already know how to swim. You start to enjoy it, *why did I not do this earlier,* you muse to yourself, *it's lovely!* However the help of others would be irrelevant and unnecessary had you not taken the decision to push off in the first place.

Improving our courage to do what's best for us starts with a simple decision, from a place of humility. *I do not know that I can't and also I do not know if I can*. What is absolutely clear however is that I will not know either way unless I act.

Chapter 9: Peace

"I lose myself here and know I am peace"

Oh how sometimes I wished to run and hide! Oh how I did run, so many times, a different country, a different job, a different partner.... this elusive thing I sought to find, a simple stability, a simple quiet... otherwise known as *peace*. For a long time, I convinced myself I would find peace in the bottom of a glass. That didn't work out so well either funnily enough!

You already have peace. Like so much in this book, we are not talking about going out to hunt down and capture something that's out there, we're talking about tapping into something that is already part of you. The only reason we do not feel peace is being caught in a web of deception fed by our egos that tries to persuade us of the requirement to direct, control and manipulate in order to achieve it.

I have made many posters on peace. Inner peace, world peace, all sorts of peace. I am a peace fan. The fundamental reason I am a fan of peace is that if I feel peace, I have no wish to harm others. We are told over and over, *hurt people hurt people* - where is the uncommon wisdom that says *peaceful people create peace*? When I am at peace I am not accidentally going to take my long held resentments and fear out on you or any other passer-by just because we happen to be sharing the same space today. What a utopian ideal that is!

I mentioned earlier that the last time I lost my temper was due to having had my sanity gaslighted. There is a part that says in such circumstances of course I ended up going mad, but that doesn't wash with me anymore, it's still my temper. I haven't lost my temper in that manner for a very long time indeed, and it threw me off track. My pride was dented, you can't call yourself a spiritual coach and be yelling at people like a banshee, surely? That's quick to deal with, I can't be a spiritual coach if I do not know what it is to be a human being and find a solution to it. Human beings get angry, I need to get over myself and I need to learn.

I do what I do in writing, coaching, inspiration not because I believe that you and I are different but because I believe we are the same. If I have had a set of experiences that have revolutionised my relationship to myself, my life, others and the nature of the divine and the universe itself that have left me content, why can't you? I also know for certain that the guidance I receive is just that, received and I need to apply it to myself as much as I offer it out on the basis it may be of service to another.

So I looked hard at myself for that anger, not because I expect to be perfect but because I know there is another way to be..... What am I saying here? I often write with my dog next to me. I write and then when I pause and re-read whatever I've written to the point where I've stopped I rest my hand on him. I can feel his heart beating through his rib cage and his fur, each little murmur saying "I'm here, I'm alive, I'm on the planet". Just like mine is beating too. In a moment of rage where's the respect to the heartbeat? Mine or anyone else's? It's not there. And that's why the anger bothered me, I did not respect the moment.

I'm getting back to peace. Like love it's a beautiful gemstone of human authenticity that exists already within, we just have to learn how to access it. Or rather we have to unlearn all the bad habits we've picked up through however many years we've had on the planet that stop us from bearing witness to silence.

Bear witness to silence. Remember it is always there, no matter how much noise you are in.

For years I have attributed the following to Eckhart Tolle "if I am capable of observing my thoughts, who then is doing the observing?". It's a question I often ask others to consider but I've researched and researched this as a quote, with and without Tolle's name alongside it and I've come to the conclusion that it's either tucked deep away in something of his I read or it's actually mine, haha. It was certainly prompted by reading of Tolle however. I can say unequivocally that he wrote, "What a liberation to realize that the "voice in my head" is not who I am. Who am I then? The one who sees that". Maybe it was my interpretation on his words at the time, maybe he's just writing something we all already know to be true and that's why it rings so...

The Power of Now I read about 6 months after I had woken up and it was a liberating and validating experience. I love to read what others write of their journeys. Earlier in this book I spoke about the need to let go of the small egoic false self in order to experience this ageless wisdom of which Tolle is clearly a teacher, and one of the examples I gave was letting go of what other people think. You can't write like he does providing wisdom and courage and support to others hoping to change and discover their true selves unless you are willing to not care what still more will say. Right at the start of this book I mentioned Angel cards (we've come a long way baby). Whatever you think of Angels, of card readings, I'll say that Doreen Virtue, who developed the pack I have, doesn't mind too much. She is doing what she loves, it's keeping her in a lifestyle she enjoys but moreover I suspect that element is just a by-product and her true reward is that when she leaves the planet she'll know she's left a positive mark on it for many. Thousands might have missed daily comfort if at the time she started receiving messages from Angels she'd sat back and thought "oh my goodness, I can't tell people I talk to Angels, they'll think I'm off my rocker". Just like courage, imagine if Martin Luther King (he appears *a lot* in my writing) had said, "well I do want to challenge racism and segregation and injustice but I'm worried about what people would think". I think great changers, great leaders, healers and transformers do so knowing that what people think is only a small part of who people are.

To find peace I must know the part of me that is beyond thoughts, judgements, fear and control. When I free myself of negative attachments to anything I suddenly discover what a contented little soul I really am. When I love myself to the same extent I would care for the sick or wounded, I am able to recover. When I stop being arrogant long enough to recognise that the sick and wounded person requiring love and compassion is me, I let go. When I can see that it's you too - I am peace. Another unchallengeable truth: **peace is within and without**.

Chapter 10: Unchallengeable Truths

When I first sat down to write this book I simply started flicking through the photo albums on my social media page, and looking at what I had made. What both did and didn't surprise me was that although there is a very clear development of my photographic and image making skills, the overall message of my writings remained unchanged over the years. As I started to write these common messages morphed into "unchallengeable truths" .

I called it **Musings and...** for reasons I suspect are now clearer - the *way* I write. It's pretty much a stream of consciousness. I hope that in writing with this freedom my journey has given me to begin to *be* me, that it sparks the same freedom for you to be the slightly-crazy-in-a-good way you, truly I do. Follow your heart! And remember;

The only change you can predict is that change happens.

There is real power for all of us in honesty, and it not is a journey for the faint hearted.

.None of us are perfect meanwhile on another level we all stand as imperfectly perfect.

The truth can never be wrong. It is just what it is.

Being equal in rights and value does not make us equal in experience.

It's good to know who you really are, and even better to be it.

Some people will treat you badly whatever you do, so whatever you do, do it for you.

In the experience of love people can do amazing things. We shall be constantly learning and changing until the day we die, things that worked for us once will not work for us always, and we can never guarantee an outcome, only what we put into the process.

Intuition is a very real experience for a great many of us, and it never tries to harm us.

There is beauty everywhere

Human beings are capable of extraordinary acts of courage.

Any human experience can be experienced by any human being.

Peace is within and without.

Thank you for reading!

Afterword

My first day after being diagnosed with post traumatic stress, I got dressed and made up, determined to achieve a little trip to the supermarket. I had become pretty much agoraphobic for a month and I knew I had to take a decision to not let it beat me. I wandered through the store, not looking really, but thinking, *"you're fine, you're fine, you can do this, just buy some milk and leave*" I picked up the milk, shaking, and I dropped it. It exploded everywhere. I stared in panic as the woman next to me looked me up and down and said, "you look like the sort who is just going to wait for someone else to come along and clear up your mess". I stood there, silent tears streaming, unable to move, barely breathing, ears ringing with the noise of my heart pounding as if it might burst at any second. There were people standing staring at me, whilst I proved this woman's point that yes, I was unable to clear up my own mess. I ran out, threw up and sat in my car for half an hour trying to control my breathing. It was another week before I went out again.

Appendix 1: A kind of Bibliography...

There are books, films and more mentioned in this book which may have sparked interest. This is not a really badly structured list pretending an academic reference point, nor is it exhaustive. It is however enough to google!

Archangel Michael Cards - Doreen Virtue
Marianne Williamson - Return to Love
Richard Rohr - Any of his many books. If you're not familiar with him Immortal Diamond, The Naked Now, and Falling Upwards are great places to start.
Eckhart Tolle - The Power of Now
The Upanishads - Eknath Easwaran's commentary and translations are most excellent for the average Westerner to grasp, not just this but his work on the Bhagavad Gita and Dhammapada also brilliant.
The Hidden History of Humanity - Youtube
Sliding Doors - movie 1998
A Few Good Men - movie 1992
Alice in Wonderland - Lewis Carroll
Blink - Malcolm Gladwell
Deepak Chopra - Any of his many books. If you're not familiar with him The Future of God is worthy start.
Rumi - Jalāl ad-Dīn Muhammad Balkhī - google quotes and works, see also Sufism
The New Testament, The Gospel of St Thomas
Martin Luther King Jr
Mother Teresa
Plato
Joyce Meyer
Rabindranath Tagore

About the Author

Heather Jane-James is a child of the 70s although she likes to think of herself as a child of the universe.

She's straightforward, kind, generous, a bit bossy, ferociously loyal to her friends and family and very funny.*

She lives in West Sussex with her children, dog and tortoise. Her website can be found at www.heatherjanejames.com Alongside her writing, details can also be found here for online coaching with Heather, artwork and more.

Praise for Jane-James & Musings**:

"Someone who has been through hell here on Earth has a wonderful insight into the resilience of the human spirit and the love that our hearts can grow to hold and know! Her story and the wisdom that has developed with it are invaluable and truly inspiring"

"She has an uncanny ability to touch the very core of your soul with her exquisite words"

"My heart is full of love for this book!! It's brilliant but more than that, I felt such a 'kinship' with you and your unchallengeable truths. I feel like I have come to those truths as well and what a privilege it is to have come to them sooner rather than later. You speak from the heart but with a clarity that people will relate to. Just wonderful. I thoroughly recommend it"

*By a friend ** By Amazon Reviewers

Printed in Great Britain
by Amazon